School-to-Home Support for Caregivers and Teachers

This book helps children grow by letting them practice reading. Here are a few guiding questions to help the reader build his or her comprehension skills. Possible answers appear here in red.

Before Reading:

- What do I think this book is about?
    - *I think this book is about Halloween.*
    - *I think this book is about children wearing costumes on Halloween.*
- What do I want to learn about this topic?
    - *I want to learn more about why Halloween is celebrated.*
    - *I want to learn about the costumes people wear on Halloween.*

During Reading:

- I wonder why...
    - *I wonder why orange and black are the colors of Halloween.*
    - *I wonder why children go trick-or-treating on Halloween.*
- What have I learned so far?
    - *I have learned that making a jack-o'-lantern on Halloween is fun.*
    - *I have learned that I like getting dressed up in a costume for Halloween.*

After Reading:

- What details did I learn about this topic?
    - *I have learned that children get candy on Halloween.*
    - *I have learned that people go to pumpkin patches to pick out a pumpkin.*
- Read the book again and look for the vocabulary words.
    - *I see the words **pumpkin patch** on page 7 and the word **costume** on page 11. The other vocabulary words are found on page 14.*

2

Halloween is here!

I see orange and black all around.

We go to a **pumpkin patch.**

I make a
jack-o'-lantern.

I put on a **costume**.

We get **candy**!

Word List

Sight Words

a	get	make	to
all	go	on	we
and	here	orange	
around	I	put	
black	is	see	

Words to Know

candy

costume

Halloween

jack-o'-lantern

pumpkin patch

28 Words

Halloween is here!

I see orange and black all around.

We go to a **pumpkin patch**.

I make a **jack-o'-lantern**.

I put on a **costume**.

We get **candy**!

My Favorite Holiday

Written by: Amy Culliford
Designed by: Bobbie Houser
Series Development: James Earley
Proofreader: Petrice Custance
Educational Consultant: Marie Lemke M.Ed.

Photographs:
t = Top, c = Center, b = Bottom, l = Left, r = Right
Shutterstock: Romolo Tavani: cover; Kiselev Andrey Valerevich: p. 1; Rawpixel.com: p. 3, 14; Aneta_Gu: p. 4 tl; Jakub Krechowicz: p. 4 tr; photka: p. 4 bl; gsk2014: p. 4 br; 5 second Studio: p. 5 t; FamVeld: p. 5 bl; MirasWonderland: p. 5 br; pixelheadphoto digitalskillet: p. 6, 14; Lordn: p. 9, 14; Nataliia Zhekova: p. 10, 14; Tijana Moraca: p. 13-14

Library and Archives Canada Cataloguing in Publication

CIP available at Library and Archives Canada

Library of Congress Cataloging-in-Publication Data

CIP available at Library of Congress

Crabtree Publishing Company
www.crabtreebooks.com   1-800-387-7650

Printed in the USA/072022/CG20220201

Copyright © 2023 **CRABTREE PUBLISHING COMPANY**

All rights reserved. No part of this publication may be reproduced, stored in a retrieval system or be transmitted in any form or by any means, electronic, mechanical, photocopying, recording, or otherwise, without the prior written permission of Crabtree Publishing Company. In Canada: We acknowledge the financial support of the Government of Canada through the Canada Book Fund for our publishing activities.

Published in the United States
Crabtree Publishing
347 Fifth Avenue, Suite 1402-145
New York, NY, 10016

Published in Canada
Crabtree Publishing
616 Welland Ave.
St. Catharines, ON, L2M 5V6